PONIES &
HORSES
STICKER ACTIVITY
BOOK

Pull out the sticker sheets and keep
them by you as you complete each page.
There are also lots of extra stickers to
use in this book or anywhere you want!
Have fun!

NATIONAL GEOGRAPHIC
Washington, D.C.

Consultant: Helen Braid
Editorial, Design, and Production by
make believe ideas

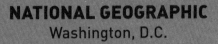

Picture credits: All images Shutterstock unless noted as follows: Bates Littlehales/NGS: 24 ml; Jak Wonderly/NGS: 1 br x2, 8 tl, 9 bl; br, 18 tm, 20 bm, 25 bl, 26 mr, 27 tl, 39 br, 40 mr; James L. Stanfield/NGS: 27 tl; Jorg Hackemann/Shutterstock: 31 tm; tr; Leonard Zhukovsky/Shutterstock: 31 ml; m; mr; **Make Believe Ideas:** 1 tr; bl, 3 tr; m; br x2, 4 tr; mr x3, 5 tl; tm; tr; ml; br, 6 m, 7 tl, 9 bm, 14 ml, 17 tm x2 (Shetland Ponies); mr (Shetland Pony), 21 bl; br, 22 tm, 27 m; bm, 29 tl; tm; tr, 31 bl, 38 l, 40 tr; **Muzsy/Shutterstock:** 34 tr; **Stuart Monk/Shutterstock:** 30 tr.

Sticker pages: All images Shutterstock unless noted as follows: Jak Wonderly/NGS: 20, 21 boots; helmet; rider (on horse); Oldenburg with rider x2, 22, 23 horse x2 tl; tr (trails activity), 24, 25 brush (brown), 40 American quarter horse mare and foal x3; Leonard Zhukovsky/Shutterstock: 30, 31 mounted officer x2; **Make Believe Ideas:** 4, 5 all ponies except Welsh Mountain pony, 6, 7 Dartmoor pony x3, 14, 15 horse x2 ll (trails activity), 16, 17 Shetland Pony x2, 18, 19 Shetland Ponies x4, 20, 21 chaps; rider (standing); jodhpurs, 24, 25 brush (red), 26, 27 Shetland Pony, 28, 29 horse x2 (find-the-difference activity), 36, 37 all horses except Andalusian.

Printed in China. 17/MBI/2

Horses are amazing!

Strong and beautiful, horses can run fast, carry heavy loads, and even swim!

Find the missing stickers!

GALLOP!

Thoroughbred

WORK!

Belgian draft horses

SWIM!

Haflinger

All horses graze on grass.

PLAY!

Arabians

GRAZE!

Sticker an apple treat for the horse!

Friesian

2

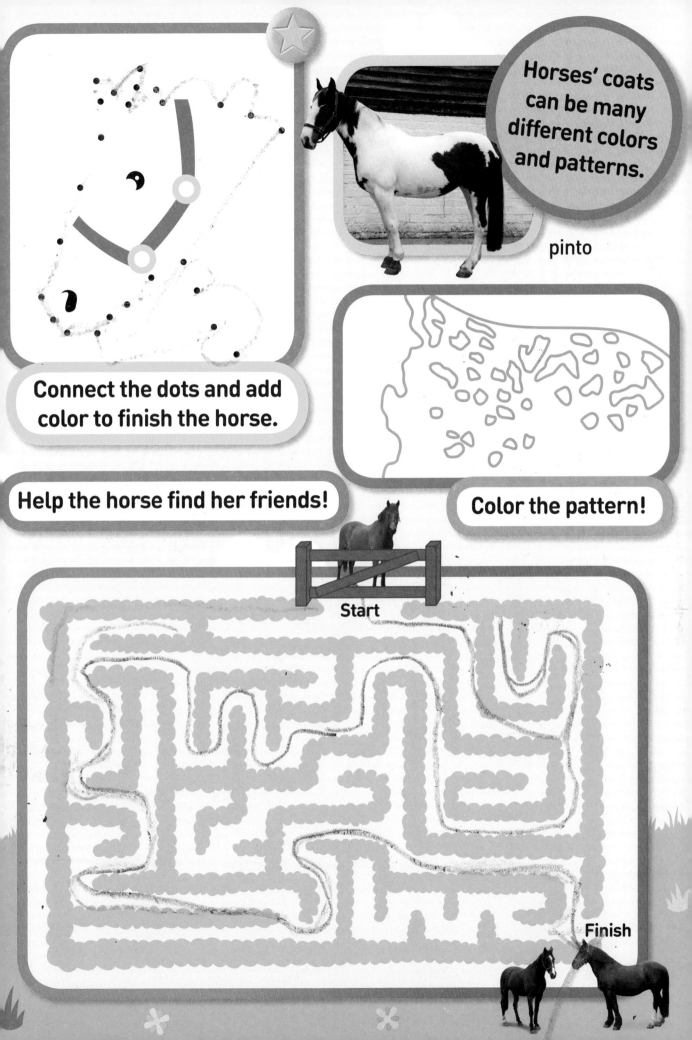

Connect the dots and add color to finish the horse.

Horses' coats can be many different colors and patterns.

pinto

Color the pattern!

Help the horse find her friends!

Start

Finish

Playful ponies!

horse → ← pony

Shetland Pony

Shetland Pony

Welsh Mountain pony

Ponies are small horses that measure 58 inches (147 cm) or less.

Sticker the ponies, then circle the one that's different.

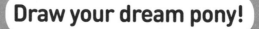

Draw your dream pony!

Find the missing stickers, then draw lines to match the pony pairs.

Despite their size, ponies can be very strong!

Help the pony find the stable!

Color the stable!

Hooves, tails, and manes!

mane

The longest horse's tail is 12 feet 6 inches (381 cm) long!

mouth

Dartmoor pony

tail

Horses and ponies walk on four hooves, which are really their toes!

hooves

Look for four horse words to finish the word search!

hoof

horse

mane

tail

t	o	i	v	h	d
a	l	h	j	o	h
i	z	d	p	r	o
l	x	w	q	s	o
f	a	k	d	e	f
m	a	n	e	o	r

Friesian horses are known for their beautiful, long manes.

Friesian

Appaloosa horses can have striped hooves!

Appaloosa

Find the horseshoe that's different!

Color the striped hooves!

Horseshoes protect a horse's hooves from damage.

Decorate the horseshoe!

7

Horse talk!

When horses snort, they may be afraid, excited, or just clearing their noses!

Draw the other half of the horse!

Large ears and eyes help horses watch for danger.

ANGRY!

flat ears

HAPPY!

ears pointing forward

SLEEPY!

ears pointing sideways and eyes closed

Find the missing stickers. How do these horses feel?

A lifted tail means a horse is excited!

Horses' teeth are always growing!

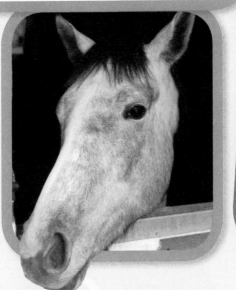

Arabian

Find the missing stickers to finish the picture.

Use your stickers to give the horses funny faces!

Sticker more flowers!

bay

What do different coats look like?
Sticker the missing horses to find out!
Hint: The shapes will help!

chestnut

dun

We describe a horse by the color of its coat. The colors seen most often are bay, chestnut, and gray.

Give the horse a pretty coat!

gray

palomino

pinto

Appaloosa

10

CHESTNUT

GRAY

APPALOOSA

11

There are many different horse breeds!

Add stickers to finish the postcard!

Wish you were here!

Arabian horses first lived in the desert.

Hanoverians and Dutch Warmbloods are powerful and easy to train, making them successful in competitions!

Dutch Warmblood

Hanoverian

Color and decorate the winner's medal!

Finish the horse patterns!

American Paint Horses are strong animals that are good at working with cattle.

American Paint Horse mare and foal

Help the American Paint Horse find the cattle!

Start →

Finish

13

Meet more horse breeds!

The American quarter horse can run a quarter of a mile (402 m) in 21 seconds!

Follow the trails to see who wins the race!

Icelandic horses are small and hardy. A heavy double coat keeps them warm in cold weather.

Add warm clothes for the Icelandic horse!

Appaloosa horses have spotted coats!

Draw your own horse coat!

Andalusian horses are chosen for movies due to their looks and energy!

Friesians

Morgan

Add stickers for the movie-star horse!

Thoroughbred

Sticker the horse breeds. Hint: The shapes will help!

Perfect ponies!

Sticker the ponies on the pony trek!

Ponies are strong and sturdy animals that can survive in difficult conditions.

16

How many different ponies can you count?

Chincoteague ponies can swim for ten minutes nonstop!

Horses and ponies can sleep while standing up!

Connemara pony

Chincoteague pony

Shetland Pony

Welsh Mountain pony

Ponies are strong!

For their size, Shetland Ponies are the strongest of all horses and ponies!

miniature Shetland Pony

Sticker more Shetland Ponies!

Color the pony and add stickers to fill the cart.

There are lots of awesome ponies!

Sticker the pony breeds.
Hint: The shapes will help!

Connemara ponies

Dartmoor ponies

New Forest Pony

Welsh Mountain ponies

German Riding ponies

Welsh ponies used to help people deliver mail!

Help the Welsh pony deliver the mail!

19

Saddle up!

People have been riding horses for over 6,000 years!

boots

shirt

chaps

helmet

gloves

jodhpurs

Sticker the rider and help her find riding clothes!

The equipment we use to ride a horse is called tack.

rein

saddle

bridle

bit

stirrup

Hanoverian

Add a rider to the horse!

Stickers for pages 6 and 7

Stickers for pages 8 and 9

SNORT!

Extra stickers

Stickers for pages 14 and 15

Stickers for pages 16 and 17

Stickers for pages 18 and 19

Stickers for pages 18 and 19 continued

Stickers for pages 20 and 21

Stickers for pages 22 and 23

Stickers for pages 24 and 25

Stickers for pages 26 and 27

Stickers for pages 28 and 29

Stickers for pages 30 and 31

Stickers for pages 32 and 33

Stickers for pages 34 and 35

Stickers for pages 36 and 37

Stickers for pages 38 and 39

Stickers for page 40

Stickers for pages 10 and 11

Stickers for pages 12 and 13

Extra stickers

Stickers for pages 2 and 3

Stickers for pages 4 and 5

Extra stickers

Use the grid to draw the saddle!

Sticker more horse riders!

There are two styles of riding: English and Western.

Find five differences between the scenes.

Terrific trotting and cool cantering!

Most horses move by walking, trotting, cantering, or galloping.

Follow the trails to find the fastest horse!

Decorate the trophy with color and stickers.

To trot, a horse moves its legs forward in diagonal pairs.

First one pair of legs lifts up.

Then the other pair of legs lifts up.

Sticker more trotting horses!

Color the galloping horses!

A galloping horse can reach average speeds of up to 30 miles an hour (48 km/h).

23

Caring for horses and ponies

Most horses are happier living with other horses.

Some horses make other friends, too!

Sticker more horse friends!

NEIGH!

Color the Norwegian Fjord Horse!

A Norwegian Fjord Horse's beautiful mane is often trimmed to stand upright!

NEIGH!

24

Taking care of a horse or pony is hard work. They need . . .

GROOMING

Sticker more brushes!

Sticker more hay for the horse!

FEEDING

CLEANING

Although many horses may never need a bath, it is important to clean their feet.

Baby horses are called **foals.**

Mares are adult female horses. Young female horses are called fillies.

Thoroughbred mare and foal

American quarter horse mare and foal

Mares and foals cuddle each other by hanging their heads over each other's necks.

Draw your own foal!

An adult male horse is called a gelding or a stallion, while a young male horse is called a colt.

Chincoteague foal

Help the foal find his friend and then get back to the field!

Start

Finish

Find the missing stickers, then draw lines to match each foal to its mom!

American Paint Horse

Shetland Pony

Haflinger

27

At work on the farm!

Horses and ponies can help with tough jobs around the farm.

Shire

Belgian draft horses

Sticker a horse plowing the field!

Finish the patterns!

Sticker the horses, then circle the one that's different.

Help the farmer put the cattle into the right fields.

Cowboys and cowgirls use horses to move their cattle.

STRIPED

BROWN

SPOTTED

29

Horses help in the city, too!

Help the mounted officer return to the police station!

Start

Police on horseback are called mounted officers.

POLICE

Finish

Police horses are trained to deal with large crowds and loud noises.

Find the missing stickers, then count the mounted officers!

Design a badge for the police horse!

Standardbred

Ready, set, GO!

Jockeys are people who ride in horse races. Racehorses can run at up to 43 miles an hour (69 km/h)!

Sticker more racehorses!

Performance time!

In show jumping, a horse and rider try to clear jumps as quickly and cleanly as possible.

Sticker obstacles to finish your show jumping course!

Obstacles are fences or mounds for horses to jump over.

Dutch Warmblood

Draw a cheering crowd!

Sticker horses and riders!

Irish Hunter

Dressage is a sport where a horse and rider score points for performing a routine.

Dressage horses' manes are usually braided!

At the horse show!

A horse show is an event where horses and ponies compete to win prizes in different activities!

Sticker horses on the podium!

3

1

2

Find more horses at the show!

Andalusian

Color and sticker the horse for the show!

Clydesdale

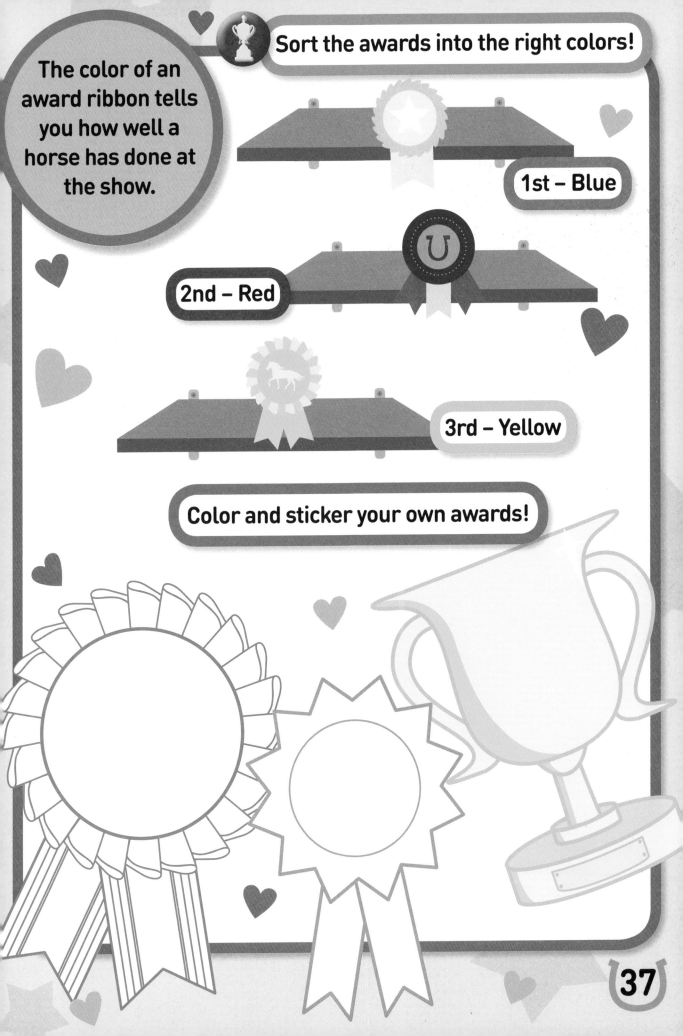

The color of an award ribbon tells you how well a horse has done at the show.

Sort the awards into the right colors!

1st – Blue

2nd – Red

3rd – Yellow

Color and sticker your own awards!

BIG and little!

Shire

Big Jake, a Belgian draft horse, is currently the world's tallest horse. At 82.75 inches (2.1 m) high, he's probably taller than your front door!

Find more big horses and decorate the picture frames!

We measure a horse's height from its withers. This is the area between its shoulder blades.

BIG!

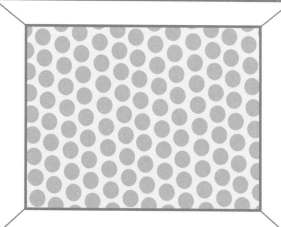

Belgian draft horse

Percheron

Clydesdale

Find the miniature horses and then see who finds the hay!

In the U.S., miniature horses can be trained as guide horses for the blind.

LITTLE!

39

miniature horse

My favorite horses and ponies!

Color the horse!

Welsh Cob

Find the missing stickers!

Draw your favorite horse!

American quarter horse
mare and foal

**Add stickers to finish
your perfect horse!**

Friesian